# Toward a More Perfect Union

# Toward a More Perfect Union

Bruce A. Lieberman

ISBN: 1547295848
ISBN 13: 9781547295845
Library of Congress Control Number: 2017909261
CreateSpace Independent Publishing Platform
North Charleston, South Carolina

*These essays are dedicated to my father, who taught me that my intellect did not make me a superior person; to my mother, who taught me the importance of distinguishing between right and wrong and always doing right; to my loving wife, Deborah, whose work with the deaf-blind is a constant source of inspiration; and, of course, to Colin, Lindsey, Ben and Will.*

# Table of Contents

# Introduction

This is a compilation of short political essays, somewhat in the style of a collection of eighteenth century political pamphlets. They are intended to help right the American ship and thereby return the country to prosperity and greatness. The essays are divided into two parts: Part One explores how and why Donald Trump was elected President of the United States in November 2016; Part Two explores ways of moving the country forward.

I bring no special expertise to this endeavor, and there are not as many footnotes as a scholar would include because I believe most of the facts presented are matters of common knowledge. You are, of course, free to disagree with my version of the facts (as well as my opinions and conclusions). My overarching opinion is that, for the most part, the opinions and conclusions I reach derive from the application of common sense. Indeed, I was tempted to title these essays "*Deciphering the Obvious*".

The essays in Part Two do not promote any ideology, party or candidate. Rather, they offer specific legislative actions and policy objectives that deserve consideration by the administration, Congress and the public. As to Congress, our representatives must understand that in considering, proposing and enacting legislation, they owe the country their independent, good faith judgment rather than blindly submitting to the demands of any party or faction. As Edmund Burke so eloquently stated:

> "*Certainly, Gentlemen, it ought to be the happiness and glory of a representative to live in the strictest union, the closest correspondence, and the most unreserved communication with his*

*constituents. Their wishes ought to have great weight with him; their opinions high respect; their business unremitted attention. It is his duty to sacrifice his repose, his pleasure, his satisfactions, to theirs; and above all, ever, and in all cases, to prefer their interest to his own. But his unbiased opinion, his mature judgement, his enlightened conscience, he ought not to sacrifice to you, to any man, or to any set of men living. These he does not derive from your pleasure; no, nor from the law and the Constitution. They are a trust from Providence, for the abuse of which he is deeply answerable. Your Representative owes you, not his industry only, but his judgement; and he betrays, instead of serving you, if he sacrifices it to your opinions.*"[1]

If we elect representatives who embrace the wisdom of Edmund Burke's message and implement – or at least give serious thought to – the actions and policies presented in Part Two, we will have made

---

1 Excerpt of speech to the Electors of Bristol, November 3, 1774.

substantial progress in "secur[ing] the Blessings of Liberty to ourselves and our Posterity."[2]

---

2 Preamble, Constitution of the United States of America.

# Part One

HOW AND WHY DONALD TRUMP
WAS ELECTED PRESIDENT

To begin with the obvious, Donald Trump was elected President by receiving a majority of votes in the Electoral College. There is no evidence that a significant number of the voting public had their votes swayed by the acts of Russia in general or WikiLeaks in particular. Nor is there evidence that a significant number of votes were swayed by the actions of former FBI Director James Comey. The only reasonable conclusion is that the majority of voters in the majority of counties, even if those voters did not constitute a majority of all voters, honestly preferred Donald Trump to Hillary Clinton. The difficult question is why?

The question is difficult because Donald Trump may be, as Fareed Zakaria has described him, a life-long BS artist; or, as Michael Bloomberg has said, a con artist; or, as others have suggested, a narcissistic, pathological liar. Because I concur with those observations, I must ask: can it be that the millions of voters who elected Trump are so stupid, so racist and/or so immoral that this is the kind of person they wanted for their President? As to the vast majority of those voters, I sincerely believe the answer is no. Nor do I believe the reason for Trump's election was Hillary Clinton's poor campaign performance or perception as an untrustworthy individual, although those factors certainly played a part. Nor do I believe that Trump was elected primarily because a great number of the middle class never recovered from the 2008-2009 recession, although that too was a factor. I believe there is a more fundamental reason: a sufficiently large segment of American voters (mostly white) were fed up with specific policies and actions of Barack Obama and, therefore, of the presumed similar policies and actions of his would-be successor, Hillary Clinton.[3]

---

3 I have no sympathy for those, including Mrs. Clinton, who blame her election loss on former FBI Director James Comey's July 5, 2016 and October 28, 2016 reports to Congress concerning the FBI's investigation of Mrs. Clinton's misuse of her personal email server. Although there are many who disagree, I believe that Comey's July 5 report was the inevitable consequence of former Attorney General Loretta Lynch's recusal following her idiotic decision to meet on the Phoenix Airport tarmac with Mrs. Clinton's husband on June 27, 2016, when the FBI's investigation of Mrs. Clinton was still open. Having informed Congress in July that the investigation was closed, Comey had no choice but to report back to Congress in October when the investigation was reopened.

At the start of her presidential campaign, if not before, Mrs. Clinton understood that her path to the presidency led through the same coalition of voters that had elected President Obama. Going down that path meant essentially three things: i) appealing to minority and liberal white voters; ii) aligning herself as closely as possible with the president; and iii) obtaining the president's unqualified endorsement and active support. While this may have been, and probably was, Mrs. Clinton's only viable option, it failed to recognize the degree to which President Obama had alienated a substantial number of white voters, notwithstanding his apparent national popularity.

There are, I believe, three major areas where President Obama's policies and actions alienated enough voters to destroy Clinton's presidential ambitions: affirmative action; foreign policy; and the criminal justice system.

# 1. Affirmative Action

One of the fundamental foundations of our democracy is that it exists in a primarily merit-based society. Yet when one examines the composition of President Obama's cabinet, sub-cabinet, other principal advisors and ambassadors, and when one looks at the composition of the crowds that attended the president's public appearances, one could not help but notice a grossly disproportionate number of minority (primarily black) and female individuals. To my knowledge, this issue rarely has been explored in the myriad of post-mortems of the election. Nevertheless, I believe there was a broad-based perception that Barack Obama had brought back affirmative action with a vengeance; and there was an equally broad-based perception that affirmative action with a vengeance was not in the country's best interest.

There was – and should have been – a place for affirmative action. That place was best described by Bayard Rustin (1912-1987), a gay black civil rights leader in the 60's who, despite being one of Dr. King's original mentors and the principal organizer of the 1963 March on Washington, never was accorded the recognition he deserved because of his sexual orientation. There are many biographical articles that assert that Mr. Rustin was opposed to affirmative action. That is not my recollection. I was peripherally involved through the Congress of Racial Equality (CORE) in the civil rights movement of the '60s, and I recall that Mr. Rustin believed that following the passage of the 1964 Civil Rights Act and the 1965 Voting Rights Act, affirmative action was a necessary vehicle for bringing blacks into the country's mainstream, *but it should be regarded as a temporary measure to jumpstart economic and political assimilation*. I do not believe Mr. Rustin would have approved of affirmative action fifty years later, and certainly not to the degree that President Obama employed it to fill top levels of government. More to the point, the *perception* of President Obama's affirmative action with a vengeance could not help but alienate a significant number of struggling white voters in the country's rust and coal belts and elsewhere.

As noted above, this issue has received very little public commentary, but I suspect its impact on Trump's election was far greater than most commentators realize.

# 2. Foreign Policy

The second area, albeit a more abstract one, pertains to President Obama's conduct of foreign policy. This is a more difficult area to evaluate because only history will judge (insofar as anything will judge) the degree to which Obama's foreign policy decisions were successes or failures. Nevertheless, the *perception* of those decisions was, on balance, not favorable to a great number of voters. It is not in the American psyche to draw a line in the sand and then walk away from it, as Obama did with Syria. It is not consistent with American exceptionalism to fly to Egypt and effectively apologize for America's alleged ill treatment of Muslims. It is not consistent with the American sense of fairness to compare the violence of Islamic extremist groups with the behavior of white medieval Crusaders – none of whom, quite obviously, was American. It is not consistent with America's moral sense for Obama's Secretary of State to effectively create a moral equivalence between: i) the firing of rockets by Hamas into Israeli civilian communities; and ii) the unavoidable death of Arab civilians (not all of whom were "innocent") during Israel's efforts to repel and eliminate those rockets. It was downright incompetent to dismiss ISIS as "the JV team"; and, as further discussed below, it was intellectually preposterous to argue that the downturn in Russia's economy proved that American and European sanctions to compel Russia's withdrawal from Crimea had been successful when Russia still occupies Crimea and is arming and otherwise supporting Ukraine's eastern separatists.[4] Finally, it was un-American in the eyes of many voters to conclude a deal with the government of Iran that included the payment of billions of dollars to support Iran's financing of terrorist organizations in the Mideast.[5]

---

4  See Part Two, Chapter 1.

5  In July 2016 President Obama argued that it was illogical to link Iran's consistent history of destabilizing, deceitful and predatory conduct with the wisdom of the proposed nuclear agreement.  In response, I posted a comment on the Wall Street Journal's website suggesting that Obama's argument was itself so illogical that it may explain his refusal to allow Harvard to release his law school grades.  In that regard, Obama's refusal to release his grades flies directly in the face of Thomas Jefferson's alleged dictum: "When a man assumes

# 3. Criminal Justice

The third area pertains to President Obama's and his administration's interference in America's criminal justice system and concurrent disrespect of the nation's police.

Many voters, including myself, voted for Obama in the hope that like many past presidents, Obama's political biases before he became president would not reflect how he acted after his election. Accordingly, we looked past Obama's prior involvement with Bill Ayers, one of the leaders of the Weathermen, which had bombed government buildings in the 1970s, as well as his relationship with his former spiritual leader, the rabid anti-American and anti-Semite Jeremiah Wright. Unfortunately, six months after he became president, Obama gave his first post-election inkling

---

a public trust, he should consider himself as public property" (Letter to Baron Alexander von Humboldt (1804), cited in B. L. Rayner, <u>Life of Jefferson</u> (1834, p. 356). The same holds true for Donald Trump's refusal to release his tax returns.

that at least some of his old biases remained. On July 16, 2009, Henry Lewis Gates, a Harvard professor and friend of the president, had a hissy fit with a Cambridge, Massachusetts, police officer that resulted in Gates' arrest for disorderly conduct. On July 23, after admitting that he did not know all the facts, Obama publicly accused the Cambridge police of having acted "stupidly".

The police had not acted stupidly and had arrested Gates only after Gates had obstinately resisted the officer's attempt to properly do his job, as Obama impliedly and reluctantly admitted the next day. But Obama's disrespect of the police in that case was only the beginning of a pattern of the president's and his administration's gratuitous interjection into purely local matters when a black person was confronted by the police.

For example, on the evening of February 19, 2012, George Zimmerman, an armed neighborhood watch coordinator in Sanford, Florida, followed Trayvon Martin, a black teenager who was walking in the neighborhood and whom

Zimmerman suspected might be there for criminal purposes. Zimmerman called the police, but before the police arrived, Zimmerman and Martin had a physical altercation in which Martin was shot and killed. After the police arrived, they took Zimmerman into custody. Zimmerman freely acknowledged that he had shot Martin. After lengthy questioning during which Zimmerman passed a voice stress analysis test, the police concluded that there was no basis for filing criminal charges against Zimmerman and released him.

On March 23, Obama publicly expressed his sympathy for the Martin family and impliedly suggested that Martin was killed because he was black, stating that if Obama had had a son, he would have looked like Martin. After what appeared to be blatant political pressure, and over the objections of the Sanford Police Department, Angela Corey, the state attorney for the Jacksonville area, decided to bypass the usual grand jury process for this kind of incident and instead charged Zimmerman with second-degree murder.

Zimmerman was tried and acquitted. Thereafter, Obama once again interjected himself, saying that thirty-five years ago, Trayvon Martin could have been him. Obama added that Eric Holder, Obama's black attorney general, was still investigating the possibility of pursuing federal civil rights charges against Zimmerman. And then, after his office concluded that it did not have enough evidence to bring charges, Holder publicly stated that he wished the standard for bringing the charges had been lower.

I have no sympathy for George Zimmerman. From everything I have read, he does not seem to be a model citizen and may very well have been guilty of murdering Martin. However, it is a sacrosanct American value that a citizen is not charged with a crime – let alone convicted – unless there is sufficient evidence to prove that the citizen is guilty beyond a reasonable doubt. It was determined early on that there was insufficient evidence to charge Zimmerman with the commission of a crime, and a president or an attorney general (or a state prosecutor) who truly shared American values would have respected those values and stayed out of it.

Then there is Ferguson, Missouri. On August 9, 2014, Michael Brown, a black 18-year old man accompanied by his friend, Dorian Johnson, appeared to have stolen several packages of cigarillos from a convenience store and assaulted the clerk who tried to stop him. A 28-year old white Ferguson police officer, Darren Wilson, arrived at the scene and saw Brown and Johnson on the street. By a vast preponderance of the credible evidence, supported by autopsy reports, Wilson shot and killed Brown after Brown attempted to lunge into the officer's vehicle and grab Wilson's gun and then charge Wilson when both men were outside the vehicle. A nationally televised protest and riot ensued.

Notwithstanding the clear and convincing evidence that Officer Wilson was entirely justified in killing Brown in self-defense, the Obama administration once again interjected itself and commenced a totally unjustified federal investigation into whether Officer Wilson had violated Brown's civil rights. The United States, under Barack Obama, thereby became complicit not only in an inexcusable waste of U.S. tax dollars, but far more importantly, in the destruction of an innocent young white police officer's personal life and professional career.

Then there was the investigation of the killing of Keith Lamont Scott, who was black, by Officer Brentley Vinson, *a black police officer*. The Mecklenburg County, North Carolina's district attorney's office ultimately determined that the officer's actions were justified. However, the relevant aspect of this incident is Hillary Clinton's initial tweet before the officer's conduct had been vindicated: "*Keith Lamont Scott. Terence Crutcher. Too many others. This has got to end*", thereby effectively pre-judging Officer Vinson's guilt precisely as had Barack Obama and his attorney general in the earlier cases.

Barack Obama routinely complained about the alleged disproportionate treatment of minorities by the criminal justice system, especially by the police, and frequently lectured the public on who we were (or were supposed to be) as Americans. While some of his complaints were justified, it was entirely un-American to use his unhappiness as a pretext for interjecting himself and his administration into the workings of the criminal justice system in individual cases just because the person killed by a police officer was black.[6] As Americans, we do not allow police officers to be subjected to criminal or civil investigation or prosecution – or, as in Baltimore, subjected to personal injuries by an uncontrolled violent mob – because a government official wants to express sympathy with the grievances, real or imagined, of any class of citizens.

As to all three of the above areas, Hillary Clinton needed to align herself so closely with President Obama that she necessarily aligned herself with what, to many white voters, was Obama's demonstrably un-American values and biases.

---

6 There was a recent report that a Trump supporter asked where was Obama when a white person was killed by the police. I suspect that many people who voted for Trump asked the same question.

The unfortunate result of doing so was that Mrs. Clinton lost the election, and President Obama's legacy to the nation is Donald J. Trump.

# Part Two

WHERE DO WE GO FROM HERE?

# 1

## Honesty is the Only Policy

Beginning in February 2014, Russia invaded and successfully annexed Crimea, not only in violation of generally of international law, but specifically in violation of the 1994 Budapest Memorandum, to which Russia was a signatory. The United States and its European allies attempted to compel the withdrawal of Russian troops from Crimea and the return of Ukrainian sovereignty by imposing economic sanctions. Those efforts were, by any reasonable measure, a complete failure because their strategic goal was not achieved and Crimea remains annexed to Russia.

In approximately November 2014, having nothing whatsoever to do with Russia's annexation of Crimea, Saudi Arabia refused to cut its production of oil notwithstanding the existing supply glut, thereby sending the price of oil to the lowest level seen in decades. Because Russia is a major exporter of oil, the oil market crash caused a major deterioration of Russia's economy.

The following December President Obama was interviewed on CNN and asked about the widespread public opinion that he had been outfoxed by Putin in connection with Russia's annexation of Crimea. In a remarkable response whose logic could be understood only, if at all, by Alice in Wonderland, the president replied that the economic pain Russia was suffering as the result of the downturn in the price of oil demonstrated that his sanctions strategy had been successful, and that neither he nor the United States had been "rolled" by Putin.[7] In other words, our president was saying

---

7 http://collection.cnn.com/content/clip/37075480_001. do.

that the failure of his sanctions strategy to accomplish its objective of returning Crimea to Ukraine was now a success because Russia was suffering from the decline in the price of oil.

Our leaders must begin to understand that "spinning" reality to avoid speaking the truth is nothing less than a version of not telling the truth. "Spinning" the truth is hardly less contemptible than an outright falsehood. In hindsight it seems almost inevitable that the habit of spinning the truth would lead to the commission of outright lies by those charged with governing the country.

An example of outright lying was provided by Hillary Clinton during her failed presidential campaign. In an apparent effort to demonstrate her courage and capacity for leadership, Clinton claimed that when she landed in Bosnia in 1996, she had to run to evade sniper fire. The truth is that she walked calmly off the plane; she was smiling and under no threat of sniper fire; and she stopped to shake hands and take pictures with the soldiers.[8]

---

8  https://www.youtube.com/watch?v=rZHO1vo762c.

Regrettably, Donald Trump has elevated outright lying to an art form – something far more un-American than anything done by previous presidents and far more typical of America's past and present enemies. Here are just a few examples: Trump promised during the presidential campaign to release his tax returns; he claimed falsely that he had won the popular vote for president if you discount millions of alleged illegal votes; he claimed equally falsely that more people attended his inauguration than attended any previous inauguration; he has incessantly lied about what is and what isn't "fake news"; and, most embarrassingly for the country, he libeled Barack Obama by falsely tweeting that Obama had wiretapped him during the presidential campaign. As to the firing of James Comey and the Trump campaign's involvement with Russia, the degree of Trump's falsehoods has yet to be determined.

Perhaps one of the most regrettable observations made by many news commentators is that voters simply do not expect politicians to tell the truth. But we cannot reasonably expect good government unless and until our leaders acknowledge that barring legitimate issues of national security,

<u>telling the truth must be their first and foremost obligation to the country</u>.

As early as the sixteenth century, the French philosopher and essayist, Michel Eyquem de Montaigne, wrote:

> *"In plain truth, lying is an accursed vice. We are not men, nor have other tie upon one another, but by our word. If we did but discover the horror and gravity of it, we should pursue it with fire and sword, and more justly than other crimes."*[9]

*Pace* Montaigne, I am not suggesting that candidates who vie for public office be executed for not telling (or grossly spinning) the truth. But I am suggesting that unless and until our leaders understand that their first priority is to tell the truth (and to have his and her subordinates do the same), it is doubtful the country's best interests will be served

---

9  <u>Essays</u>, Book 1, Chapter 9, "*Of Liars*" (1574).

by his or her election as president or member of Congress, or even as member of a state legislature.

Given the present FBI, Special Counsel and congressional investigations of Donald Trump and his associates, it is quite understandable why Trump has lashed out so violently (and so untruthfully) against the mainstream press. He has attacked the mainstream press's ongoing reporting of his and his associates' unsavory conduct as "fake news", and in what may be the most frightening example of his un-American behavior, he has called the mainstream press "the enemy of the people." Trump's war with the mainstream press is understandable <u>because this is precisely the sort of behavior to be expected by an enemy of reason and truth</u> (and, therefore, of good government). In a letter to Judge John Tyler Washington dated June 28, 1804, President Thomas Jefferson remarked that the first object in establishing whether man may be governed by reason and truth *"should...be to leave open to him all the avenues of truth. <u>The most effectual hitherto found, is the freedom of the press. It</u>*

*is therefore, the first shut up by those who fear the investigation of their actions.*"[10]

If there is any doubt about the importance of honesty in government, one need only remember that the disparagement of truthful reporting and the employment of "alternative facts" frequently is a sure sign that the government is or is becoming an authoritarian regime. The leaders of Germany under Hitler, the leaders of Russia under Putin and the leaders of the former Soviet Union are principal examples of how authoritarian regimes employ counter factual publicity and propaganda to control the population. The greatest public danger of such un-American behavior is that as the citizens of a free society become more vocal in opposing it, the usual authoritarian response is to create a national crisis. It is for this reason alone, if not for any other, that the citizens of the United States must resist the stream of outright lies that emanate from the executive branch of government under

---

10  The Letters of Thomas Jefferson (1743-1826), http://www.let.rug.nl/usa/presidents/thomas-jefferson/letters-of-thomas-jefferson/jefl164.php (emphasis added).

Donald Trump. There is too great a risk that at some point, when Trump and/or his minions are caught in one lie too many, the president, in his capacity as Commander in Chief, will attempt to deflect attention from his and his underlings' dishonesty by creating a national crisis that will, if believed, effectively compel the rest of us to rally around the flag. One of the natural consequences of doing so is war.

# 2

## On Treason

Russia is governed by a President, a Foreign Minister and a congress called the Federal Assembly of the Russian Federation. In theory, this is somewhat of a cross between the American republican and European parliamentary models. In practice, however, it is a government of essentially one person, Vladimir Vladimirovich Putin, regardless of the title with which he anoints himself at any particular time.

Ironically, our founders designed America to work as a Russian troika: three horses pulling a carriage so the carriage moves forward as efficiently and effectively as possible. Those horses are the congressional, executive and judicial branches of government. If as is now the case those branches do not work together, the government cannot move forward efficiently and effectively, and the people of the country suffer accordingly. While there is more than enough blame to go around, the fact remains that the president, along with his or her political allies in Congress, <u>must</u> make a much greater good faith effort to achieve a productive *modus operandi* with the opposition party – <u>regardless</u> of which party controls each house of Congress. Conversely, the opposition party must put aside its ideological dogmatism and recognize that it is morally and, possibly, legally wrong[11] to sacrifice the interests of the country to maintain someone's idea of ideological purity. Needless to say, scolding the judicial branch by the administration or members of Congress doesn't help either.

---

11  See Chapter 8.

It was Obama's attempt to govern through his ideological blinders that resulted in the Republicans recapturing majority control of the House of Representatives in 2010 and maintaining it in 2012; gaining complete control of Congress in 2014 and maintaining complete control in 2016; gaining or maintaining control of most state governorships from 2010 onwards; and obtaining control of most state legislatures for most of that time.

However, it is not fair to place one hundred percent of the blame on Obama. In a series of meetings that took place in December 2008 and January 2009, the leaders of the Republican Party, led by Senate Majority Leader Mitch McConnell, decided to oppose every piece of legislation offered by the Obama administration. This was the background of McConnell's October 23, 2010 infamous remark that his and his party's goal was to make Obama a one-term president.

Section 2381 of Title 18 of the United States Code defines treason as the act of levying war against the United States or adhering or giving aid or comfort to America's enemies by one who owes allegiance to the United States. More generally, treason is defined as the act of betraying one's country. Neither Mitch McConnell nor his Republican cohorts will ever be tried – let alone convicted – of treason for obstructing the Obama administration as they did. Nevertheless, in a purely moral sense, this kind of blatant obstructionism, which unabashedly placed the perceived (if misguided) interests of party over the smooth functioning of government, was just as violative of McConnell's and his colleagues' sworn duty to promote the general welfare of the country as would have been their aiding and abetting the country's enemies.

Acting with complete honesty and working together in good faith with the opposition are the indispensable prerequisites for "making America great again". For the reasons stated above, Barack Obama's biases and policies probably meant that he was not the right person to lead that effort; but the Republicans' blatant obstructionism of virtually everything Obama attempted would have made that effort impossible in any event.

# 3

## The Obscene Carried Interest Rule

Imagine this: you are a machinist working in a factory. You happen to be very good at your job. In fact, you are so good that the president of a rival company has approached you and asked you to come to work for her company. The president tells you that although she cannot offer you a higher salary, she is so confident that you can improve the company's profits that, in addition to your current salary, you will receive a bonus of five percent of the amount by which the company's gross sales increase from the previous year.

You accept the offer, you do a great job, the company's gross sales increase, and the president pays you the five percent bonus she promised. Tax time comes around, and you pay your income tax based upon your taxable income, which includes, as regular income, the amount of your bonus.

Now imagine this: you are not a machinist. Instead, you are a hedge fund manager who collects millions of dollars from your investors and invests their money in the stock market. Pursuant to your agreement with your investors, your compensation is a management fee of 2% of the total amount invested plus a bonus of 20% of the profits.

Just like the machinist, you do a good job. You invest the collected funds, a year goes by, and you sell the stock portfolio for a profit. You collect your 2% management fee plus your bonus of 20% of the profits. Now it's time to pay your taxes. Just like the machinist, your 2% compensation constitutes regular income on which you pay your tax at the regular income tax rate. But your 20% bonus

<u>is considered "carried interest", and you pay your tax on your bonus at the much lower capital gains rate</u>.

How is that possibly fair? Why does the wealthy hedge fund manager pay at a lower tax rate for doing what he or she was paid to do than the machinist pays for doing what he or she was paid to do? What social benefit has the country derived from essentially creating two classes of citizens when it comes to earning a bonus for good work? <u>As Warren Buffet has pointed out, the carried interest rule means that Mr. Buffet is taxed at a lower rate than his secretary</u>.

It is doubtful that of our tens of thousands of pages of federal laws and regulations, there is a more un-American, unwarranted, distasteful and obscene rule than the carried interest rule. To quote United States Supreme Court Justice Potter Stewart:

> *"I shall not today attempt further to define the kinds of material I understand to be embraced within that shorthand description [of hardcore*

*pornography], and perhaps I could never succeed in intelligibly doing so. But I know it when I see it...."[12]*

Without having to further define it, the carried interest rule is, like hardcore pornography, obscene. One of the first things Congress and the administration should do is eliminate the carried interest rule from the tax laws and regulations without waiting for the complete overhaul of the tax code that we all hope ultimately will be enacted.

---

12 <u>Jacobellis v. Ohio</u>, 378 US 184, 197 (1964)

# 4

## WE CAN AFFORD TO REBUILD
## THE COUNTRY

Let's start with the obvious: if, God forbid, America's homeland was attacked, and if, God willing, America vanquished its enemy, Congress's first post-war priority would be to authorize the appropriations necessary to rebuild America's damaged or destroyed infrastructure. Democrats and Republicans would unite in this effort (i.e., they would heed the lessons of Part Two's first two essays), and there would be little, if any, opposition to increasing the national debt in order to borrow the billions or trillions of dollars necessary to make the needed repairs. (This is precisely how Great Britain financed the cost of repairing its infrastructure following the end of World War II.)

Significantly, such a rebuilding effort would create an enormous addition of new jobs; much greater production from (and possibly the creation of new) American factories; and a substantial increase in the use of professional services associated with the increase in employment and production.

Because the present incontrovertible crumbling of America's infrastructure does not evoke the sense of urgency that would arise from postwar damage and destruction, it is easier for conservatives to oppose the borrowing needed to repair the infrastructure on the purported ground of "fiscal responsibility". Because those same conservatives also oppose tax increases, the country is left in a situation where its crumbling infrastructure will continue to crumble, and the likelihood of tragic accidents and deaths, as well as the cost of future repairs, will thereby increase. To put it succinctly, we are in the process of leaving a state of rubble to our children and grandchildren.

In this regard, it should be obvious that the recently enacted H.R. 22, Fixing America's Surface Transportation Act (FAST), hardly begins to come to grips with the problem. Compare FAST's annual budget of approximately $45 billion for infrastructure maintenance and repair with the $3.6 *trillion* the American Society of Civil Engineers estimates will be needed by 2020. Similarly, President Trump's vague promise of a trillion dollar infrastructure appropriation hardly addresses the problem.

Assuming, as conservatives insist, that increased taxes to fund infrastructure repair is a non-starter, and recognizing that neglecting the needed repairs will be disastrous for the country, the question Congress and the administration should be asking is <u>not</u> whether it should autho-rize sufficient borrowing to pay for the needed repairs, but rather how to minimize the fiscal impact of doing so. From a liberal economist's perspective, the question answers itself: in the-ory, the borrowed funds will be used for massive public works projects needed to repair the in-frastructure; the increased employment, manu-facturing and related services generated thereby will increase the country's gross domestic prod-uct (GDP); the country's tax revenue will in-crease thereby; and the increased revenue can be applied to pay off the increased national debt.[13]

Unfortunately, in the real world this theory does not work because America's tax laws and regulations, with their myriad of loopholes, assure that what should have been increased tax revenue

---

13 Ironically, this is essentially the same argument that the <u>conservative</u> Republican majority in Congress and members of the current administration have put forward to explain how they will pay for their still-vague budget and tax plans.

generated by the country's increased GDP will never end up in the country's coffers. While Congress is, as it usually is, debating various amendments to and/or a complete overhaul of the tax code, it is at best wishful thinking to assume that creative attorneys and accountants still will not be able to continue to reduce or eliminate their clients' tax liabilities.

There is, however, an alternative approach that should satisfy the ideological concerns of both liberals and conservatives and allow the government to borrow the funds needed to repair America's crumbling infrastructure: in addition to whatever changes in the tax code can be enacted, Congress and the administration's executive agencies also should change the country's public appropriations laws and regulations *to require that large public works contracts include mandatory tax revenue minimums.* For example, if the cost to the government of hiring a public works contactor to repair a bridge is $2.8 million, the contract could require a minimum income tax for that project of two hundred eighty thousand dollars (with appropriate holdbacks to assure payment), over and above whatever the contractor would owe for its taxable income from other projects. This approach not only would result in an assured method of substantially reducing the net cost of the borrowed funds; it also will allow the government and, possibly, the government's contractors to have more accurate, and therefore more productive, budget forecasts.[14]

Needless to say, this approach, like almost all corrective legislation, will have a hard time overcoming the obstacles of private interest lobbyists and the hard bargaining of well-meaning (and not so well-meaning) members of Congress and the administration. Nevertheless, given the dire straits of America's crumbling infrastructure, this approach deserves serious consideration. If the

---

14 Indeed, the same mandatory minimum tax can be applied to large defense contracts as well, thereby assuring an even greater increase in the country's tax revenue.

president and members of Congress have sufficient patriotism to be honest and cooperative, the
goal of rebuilding the country can be achieved.[15]

---

15 This does not mean that the ultra-wealthy should
not be required to pay higher taxes. They should do
so if for no other reason than they are the ones who
use their money and influence to lobby the government to create the very tax loopholes and exemptions
that insulate them from paying higher taxes in the first
place. As an aside, one of these days, perhaps, a sufficient number of members of Congress will realize that
raising taxes on the ultra-wealthy is the only way to
enact health care legislation that actually accomplishes
the goal of providing adequate health care for those
who otherwise cannot afford it.

# 5

## STOP BLAMING THE FEDERAL RESERVE

O ne of the most remarkable distortions of fact that have been perpetrated against the American public by many members of Congress, several administrations and numerous financial news commentators is that our economy's low growth rate is due in good measure to the alleged failure of the Federal Reserve to set proper federal funds and discount rates. Nothing could be further from the truth. There are times when the Fed can play a meaningful part in restoring the country's fiscal health, such as when Paul Volcker put an end to runaway inflation when Jimmy Carter was president. Similarly, many believe that Ben Bernanke's quantitative easing policies helped the country recover from the recent Great Recession.

However, for the most part, the way the Fed is supposed to carry out its dual mandate of controlling inflation and promoting employment is by using monetary policy to <u>tweak</u> a functioning, productive <u>fiscal</u> policy – <u>i.e., a policy based upon intelligent appropriation, entitlement and tax laws enacted by Congress and implemented by the administration</u>. Unless Congress and the administration start working together (implementing the recommendations in these essays would be a good start), the criticism of the Fed is nothing more than a feeble excuse for the fact that Congress and the administration are not doing their jobs.

# 6

## Revoke the United Nations Charter

No, this is not the rant of a right wing, America First reactionary. Rather, it is the observation of a comparatively middle-of-the road citizen who believes that political issues should be resolved primarily through the application of logic and common sense.

Leaving aside arguably important considerations such as the proven corruption of so many UN officials; the repeated reports of sexual abuse by UN "peacekeepers"; the UN's inexcusable failure to admit Germany as a member of the Security

Council; its consistent record of anti-Israel (and frequently anti-Semitic) condemnations; its admission of authoritarian and terrorist states to its Human Rights and Security Councils; and its selective disregard of its own resolutions[16], it is difficult to imagine how a peaceful world can be brought into existence when the foes of peace are legally empowered through the United Nations to prevent the enforcement of peace.

The idea that a "Security Council" comprised of the United States, France, England, China and the former Soviet Union (now Russia) could enjoy veto powers and still be expected to ensure the peaceful resolution of disputes involving them should have been ludicrous from the start to all but the feeblest of minds. But it wasn't. And to add insult to injury, the message still hasn't gotten through even after the Soviet Union's invasions of Hungary in 1956 and Czechoslovakia in 1968; Russia's invasion of Ukraine in 2014; China's ongoing conquering of Tibet and attempted appropriation to itself of the

16   See Chapter 7.

entire South China Sea; the nuclear build-up of China's client, North Korea; or the atrocities of Russia's client, President Hafez el-Assad of Syria.

This does not mean that there isn't a place for legitimate humanitarian organizations such as UNESCO or the World Health Organization. Nor does it mean that peace-loving nations should not be able to convene when appropriate and do what they can (including the use of military force) to preserve the peace. It means only the obvious: it is impossible to create or maintain an international <u>enforceable</u> legal system when a powerful member can violate the peace at will and then exercise its veto power to prevent all efforts to restrain it. Simply stated, we should stop allowing such a feckless institution to continue its cynical activities in our country while enjoying the support of our tax dollars.

# 7

## STOP WASTING U.S. TAX DOLLARS TRYING TO MAKE PEACE BETWEEN ISRAEL AND THE PALESTINIANS

There have been numerous arguments put forth to explain the failure of the Israelis and Palestinians to agree to live together peacefully in two independent states. For example, in his 2004 autobiography, *"My Life"*, President Bill Clinton blamed Yasser Arafat for rejecting the peace terms offered by Israeli Prime Minister Ehud Barak, which would have ceded to Arafat almost 90% of the land Arafat demanded for a Palestinian state. In recent years, President Obama, along with numerous European leaders, as well as the Presbyterian Church (USA), have blamed the failure primarily on Israel's continuation of its settlement construction activities. Similarly, other leaders have blamed the failure on Israel's refusal to end the sea embargo Israel imposed to prevent the importation of the weapons and materials Hamas needs to eradicate the Jewish state.

At least as to Europe, one can only wonder what explanation other than over two thousand years of government and church sponsored anti-Semitism could result in such a complete obliviousness to the obvious reason why Israel and the Palestinians cannot agree to a secure two-state solution. The reason, stated as succinctly as possible, is that the existence of a Jewish state is anathema to the Arab and Palestinian leadership and a majority of the Arab and Palestinian people. Indeed, their unremitting opposition to the existence of a Jewish state is regularly inculcated in the minds of Arab and Palestinian schoolchildren as part of the childrens' education. The supreme irony of this opposition is that while Israel is regularly castigated in the United Nations for alleged violations of UN resolutions concerning the Palestinians, a history of the conflict demonstrates incontrovertibly that it is the <u>Palestinians'</u> refusal to abide by the controlling UN resolutions that for over seventy years has rendered impossible the promise of peace.

Here are the facts:

1. In 1941, during World War II, the Grand Mufti of Jerusalem flew to Berlin and offered Adolph Hitler the services of the Palestinian people in Hitler's efforts to bring about the Final Solution: i.e., the extermination of all Jews.

2. On November 29, 1947, the United Nations General Assembly enacted Resolution 181, which established the legal and political authority for the creation of two states: one Jewish, one Arab; and on December 11, 1947, pursuant to that resolution, the British government announced that on May 15, 1948, its League of Nations Mandate,

under which it governed the area that would comprise the two states, would terminate.

3. On May 14, 1948, pursuant to and consistent with Resolution 181 and the termination of the British Mandate, Israel declared its independence. It was quickly recognized by several countries, including the United States and the Soviet Union, but was immediately attacked on all sides by the armed forces of its Palestinian and Arab neighbors, who attempted to make stillborn Israel's birth as the Jewish state contemplated by Resolution 181.

4. On May 11, 1949, after Arab and Palestinian armies failed to destroy Israel, the State of Israel was formally admitted to the United Nations as a full-fledged member state. The text of the General Assembly resolution admitting Israel to the United Nations (A/RES/273 (III)) is of critical importance. That text makes explicit reference to Resolution 181, which, as noted

above, established the legal and political authority for the creation of two states: one Arab, one Jewish. Stated as simply as it can be stated: *Israel was admitted to the United Nations as the Jewish state contemplated in Resolution 181.*

5. In 1967, the Arab armies mobilized on Israel's borders to try again to annihilate Israel but were thwarted by Israel's preemptive attack. The Arab armies failed again in the Yom Kippur War of 1973. Following these defeats, and finally realizing that a military destruction of Israel was not feasible, the Arabs and Palestinians attempted to destroy Israel by economic means by organizing (with some success) a global boycott of Israeli goods and services – in short, the ideological parent of the present BDS movement.[17]

---

17 Boycott, Divestiture and Sanctions. The international campaign to apply economic pressure on Israel to end the occupation of Gaza and the West Bank. That movement did not preclude additional armed conflicts, such as the 2006 Lebanon War and the two Intifadas.

6. In 2014, the Palestinians tried again by raining down rockets on Israel's civilian population and continuing its construction of vast networks of tunnels under Israel's territory. Those acts were committed, for the most part, by Hamas, a Palestinian terrorist group that has been welcomed by the so-called Palestinian "moderates" into Palestine's "unity" government.

And now for the kicker:

7. <u>Palestine's present leaders have publicly, steadfastly and repeatedly affirmed that Palestine will not recognize the State of Israel as a Jewish state. Indeed, as late as 2015, the Grand Mufti of Jerusalem publicly declared that there never was a Jewish Temple on the Temple Mount.</u>

*In other words, with respect to the establishment of two states, one Arab, one Jewish, mandated by United Nations Resolution 181 and affirmed by Resolution A/RES/273 (III), nothing meaningful has changed since the birth of Israel in 1948.*

Unless and until the leaders of Palestine and Israel's Arab neighbors cease brainwashing their children as to the alleged moral catastrophe of Israel's existence, agree to abide by the aforementioned UN resolutions and recognize Israel's existence as a Jewish state, no efforts by this country, Europe, the morally inexcusable BDS movement or any other political or military force will bring about the existence of a viable Palestinian state that is willing to live side by side in peace with Israel. And the real tragedy of this situation is that once the Palestinian and Arab leaders publicly recognize the existence of Israel as a Jewish state, it will be far easier to resolve all remaining issues. Even more importantly, Israel will, as it has repeatedly promised, provide the economic cooperation and assistance that the Palestinian state will require to thrive in the desert, as has its Jewish neighbor.

# 8

## Enter Grover Norquist

For all the reasons that might be advanced to explain America's present state of decline, I believe there is one reason that stands head and shoulders above all the rest. That reason is best understood by examining the activity of a person whom I have never met, although I have the greatest respect for his honesty and intelligence, notwithstanding the fact that I strongly disagree with his political and economic philosophies.

That person is Grover Norquist. Mr. Norquist is the founder and president of Americans for Tax

Reform. Through that organization, Mr. Norquist effectively induced approximately ninety-five percent of the Republican members of Congress to sign a document entitled "Taxpayer Protection Pledge" prior to the 2012 congressional and presidential elections. In that document, the signers effectively promised that as congressmen or congresswomen they would "never" vote to raise taxes.[18] Mr. Norquist's principal inducement for obtaining the congressional candidates' agreement to sign that pledge was easy: if the candidates did not sign, Mr. Norquist's organization would arrange to have them "primaried" – i.e., opposed and defeated in their Republican primaries, thus ending, or preventing the beginning of, their congressional careers.

There was nothing morally, ethically or legally objectionable to what Norquist and his organization did to induce the candidates to sign the pledge.

---

18 There were a few technical details in the pledge, but the overall effect was to pledge never to vote to raise taxes.

Indeed, that is the way our democracy is supposed to work: a voter seeks to persuade the candidate to vote the way the voter wants by promising the voter's support. <u>But there was everything morally, ethically and, perhaps, legally objectionable to the candidates' agreement to sign the pledge</u>.

The very essence of the legislative branch of our government, i.e., Congress, is that it is a place where the representatives chosen by the people meet and <u>deliberate</u> for the purpose of listening to each other and applying their <u>collective</u> wisdom in enacting laws for the general welfare of the country. The representatives do <u>not</u> have the right to delegate their legislative responsibilities to others. Yet by pledging to <u>never</u> raise taxes, they have either lied (because they do not intend to honor their pledge) or they have delegated their legislative obligation to an outside organization and have forfeited their moral, ethical and, arguably, legal obligation to deliberate with their Congressional colleagues and apply the collective wisdom of those deliberations in exercising their vote. How can an honest legislator pledge how he or she will vote on a certain matter before the facts and circumstances of that matter have been presented for deliberation?[19]

So what is the point of all this? The point is that virtually all of the problems that describe our current state of affairs can be traced to a single source: we have failed to induce our best, brightest <u>and most honest</u> citizens to devote their professional lives to public service as members of Congress and/or the executive or judicial branches of government. This may be the fault of our school system; it may be the fault of a capitalist economy that provides opportunities for greater wealth in

---

19 The fact that this egregious example of unethical and, possibly, illegal behavior applies to the Republican candidates' pledge to Mr. Norquist and his organization does not mean that Democratic members of Congress operate with a higher sense of ethics. This is just one of many examples where our representatives are far more concerned with their own election than they are with honestly serving the people who elected them – <u>in direct contradistinction to Edmund Burke's insightful counsel quoted in the Introduction</u>.

other endeavors; or it may be the natural result of a country that simply has become too divisive as the demographics of the country have changed. Whatever the reason, as the world has become a more dangerous place, and as the complexities of living have grown exponentially, we need to become far more discerning when we go to the ballot box, and we need to become far more supportive of the personal fulfillment to be gained from a life of honest public service.

# 9

## AL-SISI, POPPER AND HUMAN RIGHTS

On July 13, 2013, General Abdel Fattah al-Sisi, then Chief of Staff of the Egyptian Armed Forces, led a coup d'état that overthrew Egypt's democratically elected president, Mohamed Morsi, a member of the Muslim Brotherhood. Prior to the coup, and consistent with its radical Islamist ideology, the Muslim Brotherhood engaged in a rampage against Coptic Christians, their places of worship and other "non-believers" and their places of worship. After the coup, General al-Sisi's government turned the tables and began (and continues) a repressive regime against the Muslim

Brotherhood, its Islamist supporters and other liberal opponents of the government's repressive actions. As the result of Barack Obama's ideological bias regarding alleged human rights violations, he and his administration criticized al-Sisi, kept him at a distance and, as a punishment, suspended military assistance.

It may very well be that history will judge al-Sisi to have been as brutal, intolerant and repressive as the forces of intolerance he overthrew. But in my opinion we should withhold judgment. At least for the time being, General al-Sisi's repression of the Muslim Brotherhood and its radical Islamist followers and sympathizers is the only option he has.

This is precisely the point made by one of the twentieth century's greatest philosophers, Sir Karl Raimund Popper. In <u>The Open Society and its Enemies</u>, Popper wrote:

> *"Unlimited tolerance must lead to the disappearance of tolerance. If we extend unlimited*

*tolerance even to those who are intolerant, if we are not prepared to defend a tolerant society against the onslaught of the intolerant, then the tolerant will be destroyed, and tolerance with them. In this formulation, I do not imply, for instance, that we should always suppress the utterance of intolerant philosophies; as long as we can counter them by rational argument and keep them in check by public opinion, suppression would certainly be most unwise. But we should claim the right to suppress them if necessary even by force; for it may easily turn out that they are not prepared to meet us on the level of rational argument, but begin by denouncing all argument; they may forbid their followers to listen to rational argument, because it is deceptive, and teach them to answer arguments by the use of their fists or pistols. We should therefore claim, in the name of tolerance, the right not to tolerate the intolerant. We should claim that any movement preaching intolerance places itself outside the law, and we should consider incitement to intolerance and persecution as criminal, in the same way as we should consider incitement to murder, or to kidnapping, or to the revival of the slave trade, as criminal.*"[20]

The lesson to be learned, of course, is that the criticisms by the United States and so-called "human rights watchers" of apparently repressive regimes are not valid when they are directed against governments attempting to repress the forces of intolerance. In other words, it is a legitimate violation of a journalist's or politician's "human right" when that person is imprisoned or shot dead for opposing the authoritarian practices of Vladimir Putin; but it is not a legitimate violation of a "human right" when that person is imprisoned or shot dead for committing or inciting violence in order to destroy or suppress the lives of people with whom he or she disagrees.

The United States government, through the State Department's annual *Country Reports on*

---

20 *The Open Society and Its Enemies: The Spell of Plato*, Vol. 1, Fifth Rev. Ed., Princeton Univ. Press (1971) note 4 to chapter 7, p. 265.

*Human Rights Practices*, frequently is guilty of failing to make this distinction and has unnecessarily incurred the hostility of other governments in the process. We must lead by example. We do not accomplish much by preaching to others.

# 10

## Nation Building or Isolationism – is There a Third Way?

If nothing else, our experiences in Vietnam and Iraq (and now Syria and Libya) should have taught us that with the exception of long-term military occupation of a foreign country to accomplish regime change (such as America's occupation of Germany and Japan after World War II), America's use of its military to accomplish regime change is not likely to be successful. Indeed, recent history has proven that even with long term occupation, such as in Afghanistan, we still might not be able to accomplish the desired goals of providing the occupied country with political, social and economic stability with at least some of the trappings of representative government. Stated in other words, "nation building" usually does not work. Moreover, even if it did work, it would be highly debatable whether America's investment in blood and treasure to achieve regime change would be worth it.

Consistent with Newton's Third Law of Motion, America's efforts at regime change frequently lead to the equal and opposite result of what was intended: for the target country, the consequence frequently is social, political and economic instability; for America, the consequence frequently is an increased resolve to turn inward and withdraw from participation in global matters that do not directly implicate the country's national security. But turning inward brings into play another law of physics: The Law of the Vacuum. That law states that nature abhors a vacuum and rushes to fill it. In the real world, when America withdraws, the vacuum invariably is filled by foreign actors whose interests do not align with and may be hostile to ours, thus bringing about the very threat to our national security that we sought to prevent when we engaged in regime change.

So what, if anything, should we do in the face of the systematic murder, rape and other evil atrocities committed by other governments and non-state actors against their own people?[21] Obviously, if the evil actions of foreign governments or non-state actors appear to directly threaten America's national security, American involvement, including military action, may be the only answer because, as argued in Chapter 6, America cannot rely on the United Nations. <u>But it does not follow that America should maintain any kind of occupying force to backstop that involvement – or, in other</u>

---

21 The atrocities committed by ISIS, the Rwandan genocide, the ethnic cleansings during the Bosnian war of the '90s, the kidnapping and rape of young girls by Boko Haram and the government atrocities against the villagers of Darfur are only some of the more recent examples.

words, be responsible for what comes next.[22]  If the vacuum created by removing the malevolent forces from power results in the emergence of equally malevolent forces that are equally threatening to America's national security, then we go in again, primarily through air power if possible, remove or destroy those forces, and then again immediately disengage.  While there is no guarantee this approach will be successful, and while it may risk confrontations with major hostile powers, it is not likely to require the death and injury of thousands of American lives and the expenditure of trillions of American dollars attempting to prop up a new and friendly regime which, by historical standards, is not likely to remain friendly, reliable or even viable for very long.

The more difficult question arises when the evil atrocities perpetrated on civilians by foreign governments and non-state actors do not appear to directly threaten America's security.  What

---

22 *Pace* General Colin Powell, if you break it, you do not necessarily own it.

should America do then? It would be both presumptuous and foolish to suggest that there is an easy answer or an answer that would apply to all situations. However, I believe there are two guiding principles that should inform America's decision to become involved when these situations arise. The first principle is what I call the "Political Principal". It derives from a maxim usually attributed to Edmund Burke:

> *"The only thing necessary for evil to triumph is for good men to do nothing."*

The relevance of this maxim is that it necessarily implies that the less good men (and women) do, the greater the extent of evil. Thus, when debating whether America should become involved in attempting to put an end to an atrocity perpetrated by another country or hostile force within that country, we should attempt to determine, if we can, what other evils the continuation of the atrocity might lead to, and whether such future outcomes might threaten our national security even if there were no serious threat from the original atrocity. A perfect example of the failure to apply the Political Principle is America's belated involvement in the European theater during World War II. The predictable – and horrifying – global consequences of Nazi Germany's conquest of Eastern Europe, Scandinavia, the Low Countries and France should have resulted in America's entry into the war in Europe at a much earlier date. There can be no question but that thousands, if not millions, of lives were lost or seriously injured because we waited so long.

I call the second principle the "Moral Principle". While there may be some room for objectivity in considering the application of the Political Principle, the Moral Principle is perforce entirely subjective. If the subject evil does not appear to directly threaten America's national security, and a reasoned consideration of the subject evil results in the conclusion that the continuation of that evil is not likely to result in a future threat to America's national security, then does it follow that without some sort of international support America should close its eyes or look the other way? Again, there can be no single, all-encompassing answer. However, I would suggest that when a barbaric government or barbaric forces in another country commit(s) continuing acts of atrocity against entire groups of people, be they Armenians, Bosnians, Hutus, Croats, Jews, Darfur villagers or Yazidis, that so shock the conscience of most Americans, then it is time for America to act. To President Bill Clinton's credit, I believe it was the application of the Moral Principle that informed his decision to have the United States take the leading role in convincing NATO to employ air strikes to end the war in Bosnia.[23]

Yes, this does appear to place America in the role of policeman of the world. But that role would be far more palatable (and far more contained) if, instead of relying upon such a feckless organization as the United Nations Security Council, America

---

23 For a detailed discussion of President Clinton's decision, see the Brookings Institution's article on the subject, https://www.brookings.edu/articles/decision-to-intervene-how-the-war-in-bosnia-ended/.

assisted in the reconfiguration of NATO such that there were a new group of some NATO members and other committed allies who, by treaty, would commit to preserve the world against the acts of barbarism that the founders of the United Nations naively thought could be accomplished by the UN Charter.

Obviously, the risk of war with a major non-member power must be taken into account when deciding when and how to act. Nevertheless, at least at the moment it can reasonably be argued that life as we know it is being threatened as much by the brutal suppression, killing and torture of millions of people as it is by climate change. One would hope that Barack Obama's refusal to enforce his "red line" in Syria and the resulting murder and displacement of so many innocent Syrian civilians would be a sufficient lesson to understand the need for a more involved America in the horrible suffering of others.

# 11

## Eliminating Violent Islamic Extremism

Charles (Chuck) Colson, one of the original Watergate defendants, was rumored to have a plaque on the wall of his office that contained the following saying:

*"When you have them by the balls, their hearts and minds will follow."*[24]

---

24 That saying, or a version of it, has been attributed to numerous people, including Teddy Roosevelt, John Wayne and Lyndon Johnson.

If that were true, then it would follow that a full military victory over ISIS, Al Qaeda, the Taliban and the myriad other Islamic terrorist organizations would result in the eradication of violent Islamic extremism. But it is not true because while (and to the extent) we are accomplishing our military objectives, thousands, if not hundreds of thousands, if not millions of Muslim men, women and, especially, children are being brainwashed in madrasas, mosques and other centers of Islamic learning by the teaching of radical Islam that stem from some suras (chapters) – and later interpretations of some suras – of the Q'uran.

This is precisely the point made by Egypt's General Abdel Fattah al-Sisi in his 2015 New Year's Day speech to Al-Azhar, Egypt's leading center of Islamic learning:

> "*I am referring here to the religious clerics. We have to think hard about what we are facing—and I have, in fact, addressed this topic a couple of times before. It's inconceivable that the thinking that we hold most sacred should cause the*

*entire umma [Islamic world] to be a source of anxiety, danger, killing and destruction for the rest of the world. Impossible!*

*That thinking — I am not saying "religion" but "thinking"— that corpus of texts and ideas that we have sacralized over the centuries, to the point that departing from them has become almost impossible, is antagonizing the entire world. It's antagonizing the entire world!*

*Is it possible that 1.6 billion people [Muslims] should want to kill the rest of the world's inhabitants —that is 7 billion — so that they themselves may live? Impossible!*

*I am saying these words here at Al Azhar, before this assembly of scholars and ulema —Allah Almighty be witness to your truth on Judgment Day concerning that which I'm talking about now.*

*All this that I am telling you, you cannot feel it if you remain trapped within this mindset. You need to step outside of yourselves to be able to observe it and reflect on it from a more enlightened perspective.*

*I say and repeat again that we are in need of a religious revolution. You, imams, are responsible before Allah. The entire world, I say it again, the entire world is waiting for your next move… because this umma is being torn, it is being destroyed, it is being lost — and it is being lost by our own hands."[25]*

In other words, it is the *Muslim clerics* – <u>not</u> the western and Arab armies – that ultimately must be the liberators in the fight against violent Islamic extremism.

Unfortunately, General al-Sisi's thoughtful and profound critique necessarily leads to a question whose answer he and the clerics sympathetic to his

---

25 Translation by Michele Antaki (http://raymondibrahim.com/2015/01/01/egypts-sisi-islamic-thinking-is-antagonizing-the-entire-world/).

views may not be willing to accept. It must be assumed that not all clerics will be sympathetic to his views and, consequently, some clerics will continue to preach radical Islam. The question, therefore, is what should be done with them? Following Karl Popper's reasoning in Chapter 9 – and, apparently, General al-Sisi's agreement with that reasoning – those dissenting clerics must be, at the very least, removed from their teaching posts and publicly condemned. If those actions are not sufficient to prevent their teaching of radical Islam, then incarceration (and, in extreme cases, execution) must follow.

General al-Sisi's above quoted speech represents an ideal paradigm for Islamic government officials and clerics to work together to eliminate the scourge of violent Islamic extremism. While current military efforts by the United States and its allies are certainly necessary, the only palatable long-term solution (i.e., one that does not involve transforming the West into an alliance of police states or bombing Muslim holy sites until the "Arab street" rises up against the terrorists) lies within the *umma* itself.

# 12

## Eliminating (or at Least Substantially Reducing) Violent Urban Crime

The conclusion of this essay follows directly from the conclusion of the previous essay – namely, that progress in eliminating or substantially reducing violent urban crime[26] must, like the *umma*, come from within the affected urban communities.

---

26 Homicides and robberies, and, because of their potential for violence, burglaries.

The history of Nazi Germany, the Soviet Union, The People's Republic of China, North Vietnam, modern day Russia and other totalitarian regimes demonstrates that repressive regimes are, generally, reasonably effective in maintaining comparatively low crime rates. Stated in other words, the more intrusive the police state, the lower the rate of crime. But an intrusive police state capable of repressing its citizens to the point where violent urban crime is brought under control is not compatible with a democratic society that, like America, places such a high premium on civil liberty. The obvious conclusion to be drawn from this fact is that we cannot look only to law enforcement personnel to reduce or substantially eliminate violent urban crime. Therefore, either we must learn to live with it as an unfortunate fact of urban life, or we must explore whether there is another element of society that can render effective assistance to law enforcement. I believe there is; and, I believe (somewhat ironically) that the other element is the very gangs who are a major source of the crimes we seek to prevent.

Obviously, violent urban crime would be greatly reduced if there were a way of simply eliminating the gangs. Equally obviously, one way of accomplishing that, at least to a great degree, would be the elimination of one of the gangs' major sources of income: namely, the importation of cocaine and heroin into the United States and the destruction of meth labs in the United States and elsewhere. Because, like just about everyone else, I do not know how this can be accomplished (Trump's highly touted "Wall" notwithstanding), I would like to explore another approach.

I start with the assumptions that: i) not all gang members are "evil"; and ii) many young teenagers join gangs because of a perceived need to be a member of a respected group. If my assumptions are more or less accurate, then one possible approach to urban (and therefore gang) crime control might be to attempt to co-opt some of the gangs into community service by diverting some of the cities', states' and federal government's massive budgets for combating crime into programs that will pay gangs to participate in local clean-up, renovation and other civic programs in coordination with the local police, fire and sanitation departments as well as interested and dedicated community leaders and clergy.

While I would like to claim this as a sole original idea, it so happens that about the same time as I thought of it, which was a few decades ago, former San Francisco Mayor Willie Brown, without ever having spoken with me, attempted a watered-down version of this idea when he recruited San Francisco gang members to serve as guards on city buses. Unfortunately, the bus riders were not happy, and the experiment was terminated. In my opinion, Mayor Brown's experiment was too limited in scope and not sufficiently remunerative to the gang members to assume that on a larger scale the experiment would not work elsewhere. Perhaps even more importantly, the experiment did not sufficiently involve the active and enthusiastic participation of a sufficient number of San Francisco's municipal, fire and law enforcement personnel.

Needless to say, this approach needs to be flushed out in far greater detail and should be tried on an experimental basis in only one or two communities to determine the likelihood of meeting the same fate as Mayor Brown's bus experiment. However, if for no other than purely economic reasons, this approach should be attempted. There undoubtedly will be objections from those who say that I am advocating the bribing of criminals – or, more technically, that I am inviting "moral hazard". In my opinion, "moral hazard" be damned if it were possible to begin to invest government and private resources in such a manner that entire gangs could experiment with an alternative and productive lifestyle that could save millions of dollars that are now allocated (and frequently wasted) in attempts to reduce violent urban crime. In my opinion, the social, economic and emotional cost of allowing the present situation to continue is a cost that we, as a society, cannot afford.

Because we will not allow ourselves to combat violent urban crime by turning our cities into mini-police states, and because no one else has come up with a workable solution to the problem, I believe that just as the *umma* ultimately must be responsible for the eradication of radical Islam, it is the urban gangs, with our financial support and supervision, that must ultimately be responsible for our cities becoming once again peaceful and thriving communities.

# 13

## FILIBUSTER, CONGRESSIONAL COMITY AND THE NUCLEAR OPTION

Since the 1850s, United States Senators have used the filibuster – the tactic of talking for as long as they want – to prevent proposed legislation from being voted upon. In 1917, in order to reduce the effectiveness of this tactic, the Senate, at the urging of President Woodrow Wilson, adopted Rule 22 of the Senate rules, which allowed the Senate to end the filibuster by a two-thirds vote, a procedure known as "cloture". In 1975, the Senate reduced the number of votes required to invoke cloture to three-fifths, or sixty votes, of their one hundred members.[27]

In November 2013, the Senate's Democratic majority, under the leadership of Majority Leader Harry Reid, caused Rule 22 to be changed so that cloture could be invoked by a simple majority when debating the confirmation of most federal judicial and executive appointments. This change was called (and remains called) the "nuclear option". The ostensible purpose of the nuclear option was to severely limit what the Democrats perceived as Republican filibustering tactics to obstruct the confirmation of President Obama's appointments.

Predictably, after the Republicans maintained total control of Congress following Donald Trump's election in November 2016, the Senate's Republican majority used the nuclear option to change Rule 22 again so that now only a simple

---

27 See https://www.senate.gov/artandhistory/history/common/briefing/Filibuster_Cloture.htm.

majority is required to invoke cloture when debating the confirmation of the appointment of a Justice of the Supreme Court, thereby assuring confirmation of 10th Circuit Court of Appeals Judge Neil M. Gorsuch. Following that change, there has been some concern that the party in power may consider further changing Rule 22 to require only a simple majority to invoke cloture in debating all legislation. Indeed, Donald Trump recently called for just that.[28]

Rule 22 raises important questions concerning how to protect the rights and interests of minorities in enacting legislation. The most pressing question is to what degree procedural – or indeed substantive – acts of Congress should require more than a simple majority vote. This became a critical issue in the debates that led up to the Civil War.[29] The Constitution requires supermajorities

---

28  See  http://thehill.com/homenews/administration/335594-trump-calls-for-end-to-filibuster.

29  See, e.g., Senator John C. Calhoun's <u>A Disquisition on Government</u>, posthumously published in 1851.

in only a limited number of cases[30], and the founding fathers generally did not favor them.[31] With all respect to Mr. Madison (and I mean that sincerely), I believe there is an important reason why Congress should consider abolishing the nuclear option entirely (thus requiring sixty votes to invoke

---

30 Ratification of a treaty, override of a veto, impeachment or removal of a president other than by impeachment, passage of a Constitutional amendment, expulsion of a member of Congress, calling a Constitutional Convention, and a few quorum issues.

31 *"It has been said that more than a majority ought to have been required for a quorum; and in particular cases, if not in all, more than a majority of a quorum for a decision. That some advantages might have resulted from such a precaution cannot be denied. It might have been an additional shield to some particular interests, and another obstacle generally to hasty and partial measures. But these considerations are outweighed by the inconveniences in the opposite scale. In all cases where justice or the general good might require new laws to be passed, or active measures to be pursued, the fundamental principle of free government would be reversed."* The Federalist Papers No. 58 (Madison) (emphasis added).

cloture in all cases) and <u>expanding</u> the kinds of sub-stantive legislation that require a supermajority.[32]

There can be no question but that the United States is now more polarized than it has been since the Civil War. There also can be no question but that a predictable – if not logically necessary – con-sequence of that polarization has been a noticeable deterioration in the conduct with which United States Senators conduct themselves vis à vis their colleagues on (but not always on) the other side of the aisle. This absence of comity manifests itself not only in the growing lack of civil discourse with which the Senators deal with each other; it also manifests itself in the manner in which legislation is or is not allowed to come to the floor for a vote and executive appointments are or are not confirmed.

---

32 One might consider, for example, requiring a su-permajority for the enactment of regular appropria-tions and budget bills and, in the same spirit, abolish-ing continuing resolutions that allow the government to keep operating past the stated budget deadline. The obvious objection to this is discussed – and rejected – above.

The benefit of a supermajority is that where the two parties are more or less equally divided (and where, therefore, rancor usually is at its greatest), a supermajority necessarily requires some degree of cooperation and compromise between the two sides. Presumably, such cooperation and compromise usually will result in a greater degree of civility and comity. At the risk of being accused of wishful thinking, because some members of the House of Representatives hope someday to become members of the Senate, it is at least possible that more civility and comity in the Senate will serve as a salutary example that will inspire the members of the House to act accordingly.

Madison's argument against supermajorities, simply restated, is that supermajorities allow for deadlocks that could paralyze the functioning of government, effectively shutting government down – i.e., the same result reached by allowing an unlimited filibuster. Call it tough love if you will, but it is precisely the possibility of paralyzing the functioning of government that either will impel

Congress to work cooperatively to avoid that result or, failing to do so, will so inflame the public that a shutdown will be less likely to occur in the future. Indeed, the actions of the intransigent Republican members of the House who caused the 2013 government shutdown temporarily turned a majority of the public against the Republican Party.[33] This sort of uncooperative behavior already was evident in 2011, when Congress was compelled to include "sequestration" in the 2011 Budget Act in order to obtain sufficient votes to enact that legislation. As we subsequently learned to our regret in 2013, sequestration prevented, among other things, much-needed upgrades to the military and resulted in the loss of thousands of jobs.[34] Hopefully, those unfortunate events will serve as sufficient lessons to prevent stalemates in the future. If am wrong, then so be it. It is up to the voters to remove those

---

33 http://www.cnn.com/2013/10/21/politics/cnn-poll-gop-boehner-shutdown/index.html.

34 https://www.washingtonpost.com/news/wonk/wp/2012/09/14/the-sequester-explained/?utm_term=.c49472f98639.

members of Congress who, by their lack of civility and cooperation, allow that kind of harm to the country.

# Final Thoughts

Numerous historians, political commentators and others have described the United States of America as an "experiment". George Washington perhaps said it best:

> "[T]he preservation of the sacred fire of liberty, and the destiny of the Republican model of Government, are justly considered as deeply, perhaps as finally staked, on the experiment entrusted to the hands of the American people."[35]

Every high school science student knows the definition of an "experiment": i) the formulation of a

---

35  First Inaugural Address, April 30, 1789.

hypothesis; ii) the creation and implementation of adequate tests to determine the validity of the hypothesis; and iii) a conclusion.

For America, the hypothesis was formulated by Thomas Jefferson:

> *"No experiment can be more interesting than that we are now trying, and which we trust will end in establishing the fact, that man may be governed by reason and truth."*[36]

The interesting aspect of Jefferson's hypothesis is that he did not question whether we <u>must</u> be governed by reason and truth; rather whether we <u>may</u> be governed by reason and truth. This is not an exercise in sophistry. Jefferson knew, as we all do today, that many societies are governed by a partial or complete absence of reason and truth, which, of course, is the hallmark of a totalitarian regime. There can be no doubt but that Jefferson and his colleagues understood that the experiment

36 Thomas Jefferson, Letter to Judge John Tyler Washington, June 28, 1804, see note 10.

of a republic being governed by reason and truth would require an unending number of tests and involve far more situations than they – <u>or the Constitution they authored</u> – could anticipate. As Jefferson remarked, "*time and changes in the condition and constitution of society may require occasional and corresponding modifications....*"[37]

We are now undergoing a severe test. The test is whether the Republic can survive when so many of its leaders and representatives have allowed outright lying, partisan politics and appeals to our basest instincts to take the place of governing by reason and truth. I do not suggest that this is an entirely new phenomenon, albeit its symptoms seem to have gotten worse. I do suggest that as so many countries have become unstable, and as America's enemies and potential adversaries have become more threatening, a failure of that test has become potentially fatal.

---

37 Letter to Edward Livingston, March 25, 1825 (https://founders.archives.gov/documents/Jefferson/98-01-02-5077).

Referring to Shay's Rebellion, Jefferson wrote:

*"I hold it that a little rebellion now and then is a good thing, and as necessary in the political world as storms in the physical."*[38]

In the most benign sense of the word, a rebellion is long overdue: a rebellion in our collective thinking whereby we recognize that the American experiment in democracy is not over; we are in the midst of a great test; and we will fail that test unless we take our civic duties more seriously and become far more discerning and demanding in what we expect from our elected leaders and representatives. In that regard, we must encourage more honest and decent men and women to eschew the accumulation of great private wealth and in its place enjoy the greatest sense of personal fulfillment and pride in having participated in a life of public service.

---

38 Letter to James Madison, January 30, 1787, (https://www.varsitytutors.com/earlyamerica/early-america-review/volume-1/jefferson-letter-madison).

These essays are mere suggestions as to what we can do to move Toward a More Perfect Union. No doubt there are other equally worthy, if not worthier, suggestions. As I end many emails and letters to clients: I hope this helps.